GARIBALDI SENIOR SECONDARY
24789 Dewdney Trunk Road
Maple Ridge, B.C. V4R 1X2

NOW HIRING: THEATER

by Jane Mason

Crestwood House
New York

Maxwell Macmillan Canada
Toronto

Maxwell Macmillan International
New York   Oxford   Singapore   Sydney

Crestwood House
Macmillan Publishing Company
866 Third Avenue
New York, NY 10022

Maxwell Macmillan Canada, Inc.
1200 Eglinton Avenue East
Suite 200
Don Mills, Ontario M3C 3N1

Produced by Twelfth House Productions
Designed by R Studio T
photo credits:
cover: theater performance courtesy of Zoë Morset, other photos by Brian Vaughan
courtesy of Zoë Morset: 5
Brian Vaughan: 6, 9, 14, 17, 19, 22, 24, 26, 28, 36, 38, 42
courtesy of Lisa Benavide: 12
Martha Swope: 30–31

Macmillan Publishing Company is part of the Maxwell Communication
Group of Companies.

First Edition

Printed in the United States of America

10   9   8   7   6   5   4   3   2   1

Library of Congress Cataloging-in-Publication Data

Mason, Jane Bannister.
    Theater / by Jane Mason. — 1st ed.
      p. cm. — (Now hiring)
    Includes index.
    Summary: A description of jobs available in the theater. ISBN 0 09606-792-7
    1. Theater—Vocational guidance—Juvenile literature.
  [1. Theater—Vocational guidance. 2. Vocational guidance.]
  I. Title. II. Series. III. Series: Now hiring.
  PN2074.M37 1994
  792'.02'93—dc20   93–5744

0-382-24750-7 (pbk.)

CONTENTS

THIS BUSINESS OF THEATER

A bell rings in the theater lobby, signaling that the show is about to begin. The audience swarms into the auditorium. As the lights dim, a hush spreads over the crowd. A single spotlight comes up on the stage, and an **actor** appears. With the first few lines, the story unfolds.

Everyone loves a night at the theater. Whether it's a big Broadway musical like *The Phantom of the Opera* or a small production of Shakespeare's *Romeo and Juliet*, theater is magic.

Seeing a play is not like going to a movie or watching TV. A filmmaker can shoot a scene over and over until it's just right. But theater is live. And anything can happen.

The first plays were performed as early at 534 B.C., in Greece. These performances were part of Greek religious rites. One of the first actors was named Thespis, which is where the word *thespian* (actor) comes from.

Over time, theater became popular in Rome. But instead of serious drama, the plays were comedies. By the 1300s, plays were being presented throughout Europe. Actors performed in different towns, traveling in troupes.

Theater came to America's cities in the 1700s. In the 1800s, beautiful playhouses were built. Theater groups went on tour, which usually started in New York City. Over time, New York City became the hub of the world's theater.

When a theater production is planned, dozens of people must work together. There are **producers, playwrights, directors**, actors and actresses, and **casting directors**. There are people who design the sets, the costumes, and the lights. And many other people work behind the scenes to make sure the productions run smoothly.

4 It's not necessary to have a four-year college degree to land a job

Whether you're interested in acting or costume design or stage managing, there could be a job in theater for you.

in the theater industry. But you do need some theater skills, dedication, and patience.

The people interviewed in this book all work in the theater industry. Each person has a different job and a different story to tell. But they all have two things in common: They love what they do, and they have worked hard to get where they are. Listen to their stories, their ideas, their advice. Imagine what it would be like to have their jobs. Then decide whether you think you've got what it takes. If you think you do, go for it. Maybe someday *you'll* be behind the scenes, cuing actors, working the lights, or arranging the curtain calls.

A stage manager confers with a property master on the set.

STAGE MANAGER

Nuts and Bolts of the Job

The lights dim. The curtain rises. The chatter of birds and monkeys fills the air. The pink light of dawn warms the jungle on stage. An actor swings across the stage on a vine.

Who coordinates all this? Who makes the lights, sound, and actors operate on cue? It's the job of **stage managers** like Annie.

When Annie gets a **script** for the first time, she reads it and makes notes in the margins about the set, **props**, lights, and each actor's entrances and exits. "If there's a revolving door or 14 windows or a trap door, I make sure the **set designer** knows about it right away," Annie explains.

Annie lets the lighting, sound, and set people know about these things at the **production meeting**. "We all sit down and go over the script. We discuss how we're going to handle everything," she says.

Shortly after the production meeting, Annie gets a floor plan from the set designer. The floor plan shows where different parts of the set will go. Annie uses the plan to tape the floor. "I mark where each piece of the set will be with tape so that the actors know where things are," Annie says.

Next, Annie talks to the **property master** and gets props for rehearsals. Since she works in a **regional theater**, a professional theater located away from major theater centers, she and the prop master have access to **stock**, a collection of props from previous shows.

Another important part of Annie's job is scheduling. "I find out

RELATED JOBS:

Assistant stage manager

Property master

Director

7

which scenes the director wants to rehearse and work it into a schedule," she explains. "It can get tricky because I have to work around the actors' schedules. Sometimes an actor is working on two plays at once."

The first rehearsal usually begins with a read-through. Then the director begins **blocking**. The director tells the actors where and how to move on stage. Annie writes everything down. "If an actor can't remember where he or she is supposed to go, I can tell him. And if the director changes his or her mind, I write down the change," she explains. Annie also **prompts** the actors. "When an actor can't remember his or her line, I'm there to read it."

Throughout the weeks of rehearsals, Annie communicates with all departments in the theater. "I have to make sure that the lights, props, sound, and set people know of any changes," she says. "I'm the person who lets everyone know what is going on in rehearsal."

Just before the play opens, the director holds **technical rehearsals**. These rehearsals are devoted to working out the technical parts of a production, such as set changes and light cues. Annie writes all these changes and cues in her script. "By this time, my script has everything in it. If I were kidnapped, someone else should be able to use my script and do my job," she says.

When the show opens, Annie works from a booth at the back of the theater. From there, she **calls** the show, using the theater's audio system. During a show, Annie cues the sound and light people, who all wear headsets.

Once a show opens, the director usually goes to work on another play. Then the show becomes Annie's responsibility. "I have to make sure that we perform the show the director created," Annie explains. "If an actor wants to change how he or she reads a line, I have to tell the actor that the change is not possible. And that's not always easy."

IT'S UP TO THE STAGE MANAGER TO GET PEOPLE TO COOPERATE.

A stage manager calls the show from a booth in the back of the theater.

After each show, Annie checks that everything is okay. "I make sure that nobody is hurt and that everything is intact," Annie says. If there's a broken prop or a ripped costume, she makes sure that the right person knows about it. "I also keep track of audience sizes, reactions to the show, and how long the play takes," Annie tells us. As you can tell, Annie has her hands full in every stage of production!

Have You Got What It Takes?

A stage manager makes sure that a production runs smoothly. You've got to be willing to work long hours. You've got to be a good communicator. And you've got to be organized.

Annie wasn't always set on being a stage manager. "I wanted to be a star," she confesses. When Annie finished school, she set her sights on a job in theater.

A regional theater was looking for a secretary, and Annie got the job. "I figured I'd get my foot in the door and eventually get a part in a play," she tells us. "But it wasn't long before I realized that I wasn't tough enough to make it as an actor."

After working as a production secretary for a year, Annie was promoted to **assistant stage manager**. "I helped the stage manager in all areas of her job," she says. "It was a great learning position because I saw how things got done. I saw what worked and what didn't."

After a year as an assistant stage manager, Annie was promoted to stage manager. Two years later, the theater she was working in closed. But Annie was able to get a stage manager's position at another theater. She's been there for 20 years.

Annie likes to take care of people and help smooth the way. "You have to have a nurturing personality. And you have to be diplomatic," she says. When things aren't going well, it's up to the stage manager to get people to cooperate.

Good stage managers can think on their feet. If there's a problem, they have to come up with a solution, fast. They also have to be extremely well organized. Scheduling rehearsals and fittings is just the beginning. It's up to them to keep track of *everything* that happens on stage!

If you think you can handle all that, stage managing might be for you. Get involved in extracurricular activities at school. Offer to coordinate events, whether it's a school dance or a neighborhood car wash.

"I HAVE TO MAKE SURE WE PERFORM THE SHOW THE DIRECTOR CREATED."

You can also participate in your school or community theater. If there's a regional theater in your area, find out if the stage manager needs help. Tell him or her that you'll work for free.

Look in performance newspapers like *Backstage* for apprenticeships. These nonpaying, low-level positions are also listed in the *Summer Theater Directory*. Don't be afraid to apply for them. Once you get an internship, you'll be on your way!

ACTOR

Nuts and Bolts of the Job

A young woman stands on stage, her eyes full of tears. The man she loves has lost his mind. She raises her arms to the sky in anguish, begging the gods for help. "O, help him, you sweet heavens!" she cries out. "What a noble mind is here o'erthrown."

Who is that woman crying on stage? It's Lisa. Lisa is an actor. (The term *actor* can be used for both men and women. Women are often referred to as *actresses*, of course.) She decides how each character she plays would act in different situations. Actors draw on their instincts, their imagination, and their past experiences to make those decisions. No two actors make the same decisions about their character. That's why no two performances are the same.

Lisa gets her roles through auditions, which are set up through her agent. Her agent uses Lisa's résumé and **head shots** to help Lisa get auditions. Head shots are glossy, 8 inch × 10 inch black-and-white photographs.

Actors send head shots like this one to agents and casting directors.

Before each audition, Lisa receives the script or some **sides** from the play. Sides are the portions of the script that feature the character she's auditioning for. Lisa likes to have a few days to get familiar with her character and her lines. But sometimes the script comes at the last minute. "I might get the sides a couple of weeks in advance," she says. "But it's more likely that I'll get them the day of the audition."

At the audition, Lisa reads aloud for the casting director. Sometimes the director is there, too. "If they're considering me for the role, they also might ask me to do a **cold reading**.

RELATED JOBS:
On-stage extra
Understudy

12

I'll have to read something I've never seen before so that the casting director can see what I can do," Lisa explains.

If the casting director likes Lisa, she'll get a **callback**. A callback is a second audition at a later date. If Lisa gets called back, it means she's seriously being considered for a role. At the callback, Lisa might have to do more cold readings or read scenes with actors who have already been cast.

The director works with the actors at callback auditions. "They want to see if you are flexible and if you can take direction," Lisa explains. "Some actors have a character set in their minds when they go in to audition and can't adapt to the director's instructions."

Lisa might get a role after one audition. Or she might be called back several times. The casting director might tell her right away that she got the part. Or she might have to wait for several weeks.

"One time," Lisa remembers, "I was called back for a second audition. I felt good about the callback, but my agent and I didn't hear from the casting director for over a month. We assumed that they had decided to go with someone else. Then, a few days later, they called to tell me that I had the part! I was excited. But I had just bought airline tickets to Mexico. I had to cancel my trip!"

After Lisa lands a role in a play, the work really begins. Normally, she and the rest of the cast rehearse for about six weeks. Lisa tries to rehearse her lines quickly. This makes it possible for her to rehearse without carrying a script. It also gives her time to concentrate on her character. "It really means something to know your lines by heart," she says. "When I know something well, the words just flow out of me emotionally."

Once the play opens, Lisa performs her role almost every night. If a play is successful, Lisa might perform that same role for years. "Performing night after night isn't easy," she says. "Some nights you just don't feel your best."

Lisa says that being a stage actor is special. "There's a real connection between actors," she says. "You walk into that first

An actor uses instinct, imagination, and past experience when interpreting a character.

rehearsal, and you might not know a single person. But together you create magic."

Since theater is live, anything can happen. As Lisa puts it, "It's a leap of faith. You put your trust in the rest of the cast and crew. If someone misses a line, someone has to be there to fill in." The show must go on!

Have You Got What It Takes?

It's not easy being an actor. You have to go on countless auditions. You have to be able to play all kinds of roles. And, no matter how good you are, you have to be able to take rejection.

Lisa is a Mexican American who grew up in San Antonio, Texas. As a kid, she felt like a misfit until she got involved in theater. "I wasn't doing very well in school," she says. "There really wasn't

"IT REALLY MEANS SOMETHING TO KNOW YOUR LINES BY HEART."

anything that I felt good about."

During her junior year in high school, Lisa auditioned for the school play, a musical called *Bye, Bye Birdie*. She got a part as one of the chorus members. "All of a sudden I was doing something I loved," she says.

Lisa's role in the chorus inspired her to take drama classes. After she graduated, Lisa worked as a waitress to save money. She lived in Chicago for a while, then moved to New York City and got an agent. "Being an actress in New York is strange," Lisa says. "Sometimes I know that a casting director is considering me just because I'm Mexican. Of course, I want the work. But I don't like to think I'm getting work because of my ethnic background."

An actor has to be tough and determined. When you don't get a part, it's hard not to take it personally. It's difficult to handle rejection, and every actor—no matter how famous—gets his or her fair share of rejections. "This business can break your heart," Lisa says. "But you can't let it. You should never give up."

If you want to be an actor, go to plays and movies. Watch TV and pay attention to how different actors play different roles. Which shows or movies are your favorites? What sets certain actors apart?

It's a good idea to get as much firsthand experience as you can. Sign up for any drama classes you can find. Try out for school or community plays. If they offer you a tiny part, take it. And if you don't get a part the first time you audition, offer to work backstage. Watch experienced actors work. Then audition again for the next play.

When you finish school, find out about apprenticeships at semiprofessional theaters. Look in performing arts newspapers like *Backstage*, or in the *Summer Theater Directory*. Take any apprenticeship offered—even if it isn't acting. It will give you a chance to

"THERE'S A REAL CONNECTION BETWEEN ACTORS."

see other actors at work. If you don't get an apprenticeship, audition for roles in small community theaters. The important point is to get involved with the theater.

When you're in a play, send flyers to agents, along with your résumé and head shot. Be prepared to perform in several plays before an agent sees you. If you're persistent and have a little luck, an agent will probably decide to represent you.

CASTING DIRECTOR

Nuts and Bolts of the Job

"The sun will come out . . . tomorrow—" sings an adorable girl with curly red hair. Little Orphan Annie captured audiences night after night when the musical show *Annie* was playing on Broadway. The kid was a heartbreaker, so perfect for the role she could have been born to play it!

Who makes sure that each actor is just right for the role he or she plays? Casting directors like Daniel. Daniel is responsible for casting all the actors in a play. As he puts it, "My job is to get the best possible cast for every play I work on."

One big part of Daniel's job is knowing the abilities of actors. There are hundreds of new actors trying to break into the business every year. Daniel tries to see as many of these actors as possible. "I usually go to the theater between two and five times a week," he says. He also goes to movies and watches for new faces on TV.

The first thing Daniel does when he's casting a play is to read the

A casting director reviews head shots when trying to cast a play.

script. "I read a script and try to imagine which actors I see in the roles," he says. Daniel makes a list of actors he thinks are suitable for each part. For a play with ten people in the cast, Daniel might have 15 pages of lists!

Next, Daniel talks to the playwright and the director to see how they envision the play. "I have to satisfy the director's and the playwright's visions," Daniel explains. "Sometimes those visions are different, so I have to be flexible and offer a lot of suggestions."

The director might know exactly who he or she wants to cast in certain roles. Famous actors are usually offered roles over the phone. They don't have to audition. When stars aren't being used, Daniel calls the agents of all the actors on his list to see if they are available and interested in the parts.

If an agent thinks the role is right for the actor, the agent will set

"SOME ACTORS AUDITION WELL, AND OTHERS DON'T."

up an audition. During these auditions, Daniel tries to make the actors feel comfortable so that they can give their best performance. "I have to be friendly so that the actors connect with me and the part they're reading for," he says.

Daniel looks for certain things during auditions. Does the actor's voice carry? Does the actor seem natural while performing? Is he or she believable in the role? How will the actor fit in with the rest of the cast?

After the first round of auditions, Daniel calls back the actors he's interested in. The director is always at callback auditions. He or she works with the actors to see how they take direction. "Some actors audition well, and others don't," says Daniel. "But a little coaching from the director can really help an actor do a good job."

After one or two callback auditions, Daniel and the director decide who will be in the cast. They choose the best actor for each role. But sometimes they disagree. "I don't make the decisions," Daniel says. "The director has the final say. But I always offer my opinion. And if I feel strongly about an actor, I will say so."

RELATED JOBS:
Director
Assistant casting director
Producer
Artistic director

Have You Got What It Takes?

A casting director has a lot to coordinate. You have to understand the director's vision of the play. You have to select actors who can play each part. And you have to watch and listen carefully to countless auditions.

Daniel grew up in New York City. As a child, he went to the theater whenever he could. He was also active in shows at school. "I was always in plays at school and camp," he recalls. "When I was about 12, I knew I wanted to make theater a career." But he wasn't sure what part of the theater industry interested him the most.

Some casting directors hold auditions in their offices.

When Daniel finished high school, he got an internship at a small theater in New York. The theater management was looking for an assistant, and Daniel got the position. While working, Daniel learned how all the different areas of theater work.

Eventually, Daniel worked his way up to a full-time, paying position. By then he knew that he wanted to get involved in casting. So he began assisting the casting director. "I made phone calls to agents and actors and set up auditions," says Daniel.

After a while, Daniel got a job as casting director at an organization in New York that casts plays for nonprofit theaters all over the country. He worked there for about five years. Then he was hired as casting director at an off-Broadway theater company. Now he's the casting director at Lincoln Center Theater in New York.

A good casting director has a lot of patience and is diplomatic. "People can be difficult and demanding," Daniel explains. "I have to be able to express my thoughts without offending anyone." Casting directors communicate with all kinds of people, from sensitive actors to artistic directors to pushy agents.

19

Are you interested in becoming a casting director? "Go to the theater as much as you can," Daniel advises. Whenever there's a play in your community, attend. Watch how the characters interact. See if the actors fit the roles they play.

"You should also get involved in school or community theater," Daniel says. Getting involved in a production takes the mystery out of stage performance. Find out if school or community directors (many won't have casting directors) want help at auditions.

It's also a good idea to read as many scripts as you can. Your school and local libraries have many great plays that you can borrow and read. "The more plays you are familiar with," Daniel says, "the better."

SET DESIGNER

Nuts and Bolts of the Job

The set for the play takes your breath away. In fact, when the curtain opens to reveal it, the audience claps! A complicated network of catwalks runs across the stage. A small boat seems to float over the floor. And an eerie, white mist covers the stage, giving the illusion of water.

Who created this magic? Who designs sets that take your breath away? It's the work of set designers like Diane.

Diane works on Broadway plays in New York City. For the plays she works on, she designs everything that you see around or behind the actors. "That includes the **backdrops**, the furniture—

everything," says Diane. Backdrops are panels of wood and canvas that are hung at the back of the stage.

When Diane is hired to do the set for a show, she starts by reading the script. Then she meets with the director, the stage manager, and the **lighting designer** to talk about the show. "It's like a powwow," explains Diane. "The director tells us how he or she envisions the show. Then the lighting designer and I explain our ideas."

RELATED JOBS:
Set carpenter
Scenic artist
Property master
Assistant set designer

Diane talks to the director until she feels she has a good understanding of what he or she wants. Then she draws up some sketches. "I draw out how I imagine the set," Diane says. "I try to be detailed so that my ideas are clear from the very beginning."

When Diane is satisfied with the sketches, she shows them to the director. If he or she likes the approach Diane has taken, the sketches are approved.

After sketch approval, Diane makes a model of her set. The model is a tiny replica of the finished set. "Since I don't build the sets myself, I want the people who do to know exactly what I want," Diane says. "So I build as many details into the model as I can."

Once the director has approved the model, Diane does a technical drawing of the set design. The technical drawing features the exact dimensions of everything in the set.

Next, Diane gets bids from several **scene shops**. Scene shops specialize in building sets. Diane shows each shop the sketches

"I BUILD AS MANY DETAILS INTO THE MODEL AS I CAN."

A set designer drafts ideas for a new set.

and the model. She also gives the shops information like what kind of paint she wants on the walls.

The shops decide how much they'll charge to build the set. Then, a representative from each shop bids for the job. "The bids tend to be totally different. One shop might say it'll build the set for $87,000. Another will say $195,000," Diane explains. "Since I've been in the business for a while, I know most of the shops and their work. But we usually go with someone who bids in the middle."

A shop takes about a month to build a basic set. Elaborate sets take longer. "On average, I make about six trips to the shop during production," Diane says. "But if the set has something complicated, like a spiral staircase or a swimming pool, I'll make more trips to make sure production goes smoothly."

When the set is finished, it's **loaded in**, or moved into the theater. "It generally takes about two days. Some sets have a zillion pieces. Others are pretty simple," Diane says.

During setup week, Diane works from 8 A.M. to 8 P.M. every day. She has to be there to make sure the set is assembled properly. She also has to supervise the furniture and prop setup. The entire set is her responsibility.

Now it's time for technical rehearsals. During these rehearsals, the actors run through the production, stopping to insert light cues and set changes. "We might decide that a trapdoor isn't working or that we want more pictures on the walls," Diane says. "During technical rehearsals the final touches are applied to the set."

Have You Got What It Takes?

A set designer has to come up with a new design for every show. They have to sketch and build detailed models. They have to work well with designers, directors, stage managers, and carpenters. And they have to be available at all times for adjustments and changes. If you're creative *and* detail-oriented, then set designer could be the job for you!

Diane got into theater when she was a freshman in high school. "I used to help build and paint sets," she tells us. "A lot of my friends were in the theater, and we had fun working backstage." By the time Diane was a sophomore, she was in charge of school sets.

Diane's professional career began in New York City. She got a position as an apprentice with a well-known set designer. "I ran errands, went to the theater a lot, and worked on models in the studio," Diane says. That early experience with models has been very valuable. "If you know how to build a good model, your set designs have a better chance of turning out well."

Diane worked as an apprentice for several years. During that

"ON AVERAGE, I MAKE ABOUT SIX TRIPS TO THE SHOP."

A set designer tries to be as detailed as possible when building a model.

time, she did **free-lance** work on the side, helping design sets for different theaters. Eventually she became a full-time set designer.

Does Diane's job sound interesting? If set design appeals to you, sign up for some studio art classes at school. Any class will be helpful, but drawing, design, and ceramics are especially useful.

You'll also want to learn how sets are built. Volunteer to paint sets backstage, as Diane did. If you follow her path, you could be a set designer, too!

PROPERTY MASTER

Nuts and Bolts of the Job

In the first scene, 12 glamorous young dancers carry hot pink telephones. They briefly alight on 12 glittering gold chairs. Then they sip from 12 crystal goblets. Pink telephones! Gold chairs?

Who finds these objects? Who makes sure that everything looks just right and is in the right place at the right time—every night? It's the job of property masters like David. David works for a theater in Connecticut. He is responsible for props on the set.

David spends a lot of time hunting for items to be used in plays. He gets props in antique shops, thrift stores, junk shops, and at flea markets. But before he hits the road in search of props, David reads the script carefully. "Playwrights almost always mention props in the script," David explains. He makes a note of each item listed. He also writes down prop ideas that come to him.

Then David meets with the set designer. Together they decide if they are going to go with the props in the script. "We might feel that there are too many props mentioned. Or we might have ideas for different kinds of props," he says.

Props are broken down into four categories. Things like couches and rugs are scene props. Hand props are items that are handled by the actors, like letters or coffee cups. Dress props include curtains, mirrors, and lamps. And fog, doorbells, and shattering glass are effects.

David makes a list of the props that he needs to purchase. He might spend weeks on the phone and on the road searching for just a few items.

David also has a list of pull items. Pull items are objects that a theater has in stock. A prop is almost always saved and reused. If

Sometimes a property master builds props for theater productions.

an item is on hand in the stock collection, it saves David time and money.

Sometimes David and his staff build props for plays. "It's getting harder and harder to find good props. I used to be able to get lots of props at Goodwill. Now I can't even find them at antique shops," David laments. "So I have to work with what I have or create something new."

When David is getting the props for a show together, he has what he calls a **touchstone piece**. "It's the single prop that represents the show and the props I want to put in it," David explains. "It can be anything. But every other prop goes back to that object. It's the center of all the props."

David likes to give the actors their props as close to the first rehearsal as possible. "They have to feel comfortable with everything so that they can focus on their lines," David explains. "If I don't have the right wheelchair, I fix something up that's close to the one I plan to use."

During each performance of the play, David **runs props**. That means he makes sure that each prop is in the right place at the right time. There's a prop table backstage, where actors return their props after they've used them. David makes sure that the actors do just that. And he replaces props on the stage between scenes.

David enjoys being a property master. "I have a real love of things," he says. "Junk shopping has always been something that I love to do."

David also enjoys being able to work one-on-one with almost everyone involved in the production—the actors, the set designer, the director, the producer, and the stage manager. "Sometimes it's rough, because they all want something from you," he says. "They can demand any kind of prop, and you have to get it for them. That's your job, to make sure they feel comfortable with every prop."

RELATED JOBS:
Set designer
Stage manager

Have You Got What It Takes?

Good property masters know, for example, what kind of gas fixtures people used in 1880. And what a hotel telephone booth looked like in 1928. They know where to get props quickly and cheaply. And if a prop isn't available, they know how to make it.

David has always had the makings of a prop master. "When I was young, I developed a love of objects," he tells us. "I always wanted to know what things were used for and how they were made."

In high school, David got involved in his school's theater program. First he acted in a couple of plays. "Then I started working on the crews. I moved scenery and ran flies," he says. Running flies means operating the **fly system,** which lifts scenery clear of the stage.

When David finished school, his job search led him to community theaters and **summer stock** in Ohio. He also worked with the New York City Opera during its summer seasons. Eventually he was hired by the Connecticut theater where he works now.

A property master pulls props from stock.

Although David has been doing props for many years, he is still learning. When you design a set for a historical play, the props have to be accurate for the time period. "I am constantly doing research," David says. "To do my job, you have to figure out how people lived so that you can represent it on stage."

A good props person must be able to tell when and how an item was made. Was that lamp mass-produced or was it made in limited quantities? Is that telephone from the early 1900s or the 1950s? What material is that tablecloth made of—cotton, linen, or polyester? A good props person can answer all of these questions.

It's also important that you have a flair for design. Props have to look authentic; they also have to look right with the set and the costumes. When you're out on the road in search of a certain piece, you have to keep all the other props in mind. "I'm creating a living world on the stage. And it needs to look real," says David.

If you'd like to be a props person, "Never stop looking and seeing," David advises. Go to junk shops and thrift stores. Make a list of the things you find. Or go to the library and check out some books on antiques.

When you go to a play or movie or watch TV, notice the props in the background. Do they look real? Do they fit with everything else on the set?

You might be able to work on props for your school theater production. Since school budgets are usually limited, it will be a challenge. Learn how to find bargains at secondhand stores. Ask store owners if you can use their objects in exchange for credit on the program. See how many props you can get for free!

"I'M CREATING A LIVING WORLD ON THE STAGE."

FIGHT DIRECTOR

Nuts and Bolts of the Job

A sword slashes through the air. The actors dart and lunge across the stage, each trying to avoid the pierce of the other's sword. Finally, one man knocks his opponent's weapon away. In a flash, he pins the man to the ground, a sword pointing at his chest. The fight is over.

A fight scene must be practiced so that the actors involved don't get hurt.

Who stages incredible fights like this one? It's the job of **fight directors** like Mike. Mike **choreographs** fights and stunts for theater performances. That means he thinks up the movements and details of the fight scenes and teaches them to the actors. Mike has his own stunt school. He works with a team of nine people. When a play requires fights or stunts, a fight director like Mike is hired to work out the tricky action scenes.

First the director sends the script to Mike. "I read it and outline the violent movements," says Mike. "I make notes. I think about the characters in the fight scenes and why they are being violent.

And I note the physical characteristics of the actors. Are they big or small, athletic or scrawny, male or female? All of these things help determine how I set up a fight."

Using his notes, Mike plans out the **footworks** for the fights. He figures out exactly where each actor will step, and when. "I usually do at least two different versions of each fight so that the director and the cast have a choice," he explains.

Once Mike has the basic steps worked out, he shows them to his stunt team. The team tries it out to see how it works. "We perform everything as if we're the actors," says Mike. "We work on each version of a fight until we think it's working well." Mike likes to be sure that a fight looks natural and exciting before he shows it to the director. But he also has to be positive that the moves are safe. "With fights, safety is my number one concern," he says.

RELATED JOBS:
Choreographer
Stunt person

Next, Mike and his team meet with the director. "We show the director what we've done, and hopefully one of the versions is what he or she had in mind," he says. If it is, Mike and his team demonstrate the moves to the actors. "That's when we watch jaws drop," he laughs. "Someone always says, 'Oh, my gosh, I have to do *that?*'"

Mike and the team work with the actors, teaching them the moves. First the actors learn the foot movements. Then they work on breathing. Breathing is important because actors often have to recite lines and fight at the same time. It's important that they don't sound out of breath. Once the actors are comfortable with the foot moves and the breathing, they add the other fight moves.

"WITH FIGHTS, SAFETY IS MY NUMBER ONE CONCERN."

Sometimes, movements are tailored for actors. "If an actor doesn't feel comfortable with part of the fight, we change it," Mike explains. "It's essential that everyone feels confident with every single move."

The cast does most of its rehearsing, including fight work, in a rehearsal space. When it's close to opening night, the rehearsals move to the stage. "Once we get on stage, things really come together," Mike tells us. "We have the lights, the set, the real props. But sometimes we have to rework parts of the fight because they don't come out as planned on the stage."

The last thing Mike teaches the actors is an escape technique for each fight. "Escape techniques are used when something goes wrong," he explains. "The show must continue, and *everyone*—the light people, the sound people, the cast—has to know what to do."

The escape technique is usually a simple visual or vocal cue. "It might be a line or the way an actor holds his arm," Mike says. The cue lets everyone know that there's a problem. Once the cast and crew know what is happening, they can adjust and do what's necessary to keep the play going smoothly.

Although unexpected events sometimes occur, they're usually not serious. "In all my years of fight directing, I've never had a serious injury happen in one of my fights," Mike says proudly. "I take safety very seriously. If someone isn't capable of doing a move, then he or she just shouldn't do it. It's not worth the risk."

Have You Got What It Takes?

A fight director has to be in great shape. Those moves aren't easy! You need to be creative. You need to be able to work well wih people. And you have to be guided by safety techniques and procedures. Think you can handle it? Mike can!

Mike grew up in Connecticut and has always been a natural athlete. "I started taking gymnastics when I was seven or eight," he says. "And I played a lot of baseball and football."

But Mike's talent extended past athletics. He started acting back in kindergarten. He tried all kinds of roles but found his niche in comedy. He loved parts that were funny and involved a lot of movement. "I've always loved watching Charlie Chaplin and Wild West movies," he says.

By high school, Mike knew that he wanted to get into stunt work. Then a bad accident almost cost him his leg and his dream. But Mike was determined. And after two years of rehabilitation, he was ready to enroll in a stunt school. "It was an eight-week course that taught me all about performing stunts and staging fights," he says. When he finished the course, Mike was a certified **stunt person**. He worked for several years with that same stunt school. Then he started his own school.

Mike says that his school is successful because he likes to work with people. This is an important quality for a fight director to have. "I try hard not to insult the integrity of an actor," Mike tells us. "And sometimes I have to tell actors that they can't do a certain move or that they're being too aggressive. That's not easy."

Are you interested in becoming a fight director? "It's extremely important that you're in good shape, both physically and mentally," Mike says. "You have to have good body control. But you also have to have a good mind-set, a positive attitude."

So get yourself in shape. Work out as often as you can—run, swim, bike, lift weights. And work on coordination. Aerobic classes are good for that. Classes in boxing, dance, or fencing will be helpful, too.

Remember, Mike started out acting! So get out there and audition for school plays. Go for roles that are physical. If you get a chance to be in fight scenes, pay careful attention to how the fight director works. Ask questions about the moves. Learn as much as you can.

"Most of all, go for it," Mike says. "If you work hard and discipline yourself, you can do it!"

COSTUME DESIGNER

Nuts and Bolts of the Job

The spotlight illuminates an actress at center stage, and her costume is dazzling. Colored feathers surround her head like a halo. Rhinestones and pearls glimmer from the bodice of her gown. And as she moves, her wide hoopskirt sweeps the floor like a giant bell.

Who creates lavish costumes like this for the theater? **Costume designers** like Teresa do. Teresa designs the clothing in the plays she works on, from shoes to skirts to hats.

Like almost everyone who works in theater, Teresa begins her job by reading the script. "While I read, I think about costume ideas," she says. Then Teresa meets with the director to find out what ideas he or she has for costumes. If it's a new play, the playwright might also attend the meeting. By the time the meeting is over, Teresa is ready to get to work.

Teresa uses her collection of costume and clothing books to research costumes for a play. She also uses files that are full of pictures of different kinds of clothes. "I have files of clothes from different countries, time periods, and shows I've done," she explains.

Teresa uses the files to create **picture boards**—poster-sized boards with pictures glued onto them. Each major character in a play usually has his or her own board. "The boards are important. Since I work in images, I need to talk in images," Teresa explains. "The director needs to *see* what kinds of costumes I'm thinking about."

Using the boards, Teresa and the director choose basic ideas for costumes. Then Teresa sketches out each piece of clothing. "If there's a debate about color, I'll photocopy a sketch several times

A costume designer works with a seamstress in a costume shop.

and paint it different colors so that we can decide which color is best," Teresa says.

Then Teresa buys fabric samples for the costumes. Sometimes the director wants to see the materials Teresa is going to use. At other times the final decision is Teresa's.

"SINCE I WORK IN IMAGES, I NEED TO TALK IN IMAGES."

If the play Teresa is working on is for a regional theater, the theater has its own costume shop where the clothing is made. If she's working on a Broadway show, Teresa gets bids from outside costume shops.

About the time Teresa decides who will make the costumes, the director holds the first rehearsal. Teresa is there to hear the script being read and to get a feeling for the play. She also takes the actors' measurements. "If an actor is taller or shorter or heavier than I thought, I'll change the costume designs," she says.

When the costumes are ready, Teresa oversees the fittings. Everything has to fit just right. And the costumes need to suit the movements the actors will make on stage. "If the director has them making strange movements, I have to make sure the costumes allow for these movements," she explains.

When the costumes are finished, they're viewed under the stage lights. This is the time for Teresa to make last-minute changes. "When you see the costumes on stage with the lights and the set, they often look different from what you expected," Teresa says. She might decide to dye a costume to make it look more dramatic under the lights. Or she might have to fix a hem on the bottom of a skirt. There are always a few last-minute adjustments.

If necessary, the costumes are also **rigged**. Rigged costumes are easier to get on and off. "Actors often have to change costumes very quickly. So we might put snaps behind the buttons on a shirt. Or we'll use Velcro instead of a pants zipper." When you have to change clothes fast, every button counts!

A costume designer makes adjustments to a nearly completed costume.

Have You Got What It Takes?

Costume designers do more than design costumes. They coordinate the creation of them, too. They make decisions about fabrics. And they make alterations in every stage of a show's production.

Teresa has always been interested in clothing. When she was six, she was sewing by hand. By the time she was ten, she was designing and sewing clothes for her Barbie dolls.

In junior high and high school, Teresa got involved in the theater.

She acted in plays and helped out behind the scenes. "I painted sets and things like that," she says. "We were also in charge of making our own costumes. They weren't very complicated. But they were costumes."

When Teresa was in high school, she realized how much she enjoyed arts and crafts. She decided to pursue theater and got an internship with a famous Broadway costume designer in New York.

While interning, Teresa "did everything from getting coffee and art supplies to researching costumes." But the most important part of Teresa's intern experience was being able to watch designers work. "I learned a lot from just seeing," she says.

Since Teresa's internship didn't pay anything, she needed another job. Her boss helped her get a part-time position as a **wardrobe assistant** at a small theater in New York City. "I handled the costumes for the show four nights a week," Teresa says. "That meant washing out stockings, sending dresses and suits to the dry cleaners, and ironing." It wasn't very glamorous, but it gave Teresa some great experience!

Are you interested in becoming a costume designer? "Take art classes, including figure drawing," Teresa advises. Find out what kind of classes are offered at your school or the local community college. Buy some drawing pencils and start sketching—especially people and clothes.

Learn how to sew. Take home economics at school. If you have a sewing machine at home, learn how to use it. Start with simple projects, like an apron, and work up to harder things. When you shop for fabrics, pay attention to the way different materials look and feel.

You can also apply for summer internships with regional theaters. Look in the *Summer Theater Directory* for theaters. Then apply for an apprenticeship working with costumes. The job may be the beginning of a career!

FOUR THINGS TO REMEMBER NO MATTER WHAT THEATER JOB YOU WANT

1. Do your homework.

Soak up information about the theater job you're interested in. If you know what you're talking about, people will be more likely to give you a job.

Also, do a little research. Check your local library for books on the theater industry. Your school career counselor may know where you can get more information. So be sure to ask.

2. Reach out to people in the business.

If there's a community or regional theater in your town, call the office. Tell the person you talk to that you're interested in getting into theater. Ask if the theater is hiring assistants. If not, say that you'll work for free.

Next, type up a résumé. Include your name, address, phone number, and anything you've done that makes you a good person to hire. Be sure to list any theater experience you have had. That includes small roles in school plays and volunteer work at local theaters. If you have any special skills, like basic carpentry or sewing, be sure to put that on your résumé, too. A sample résumé can be found at the end of this chapter.

When you apply for a position, send your résumé, along with a cover letter, to the theater company. A cover letter is a brief note asking that you be considered for a job. Try to get the name of the theater's producer or artistic director. Address your letter to him or her.

When you go for an interview, wear appropriate clothes. Speak clearly when you answer the interviewer's questions. Be upbeat and positive. And give the message that you're not afraid to work hard.

3. Find a mentor.

Get to know someone who can teach you about the theater industry. If you're a theater buff, you may already know someone who works in the field. If possible, watch him or her on the job. Ask questions. And most important, let that person know you want to get into theater. Your mentor might introduce you to other people in the industry.

4. Work your way up.

Take any position in the theater you can get. You may not earn a salary. And you may have to start with a job that doesn't thrill you. But you'll gain experience doing it.

Once you get a position, work hard and learn as much as you can. Watch the people around you. See how they work. Offer to help out whenever you can. If a higher position comes up that you'd like to be considered for, tell your boss that you're interested. Even if he or she doesn't think you're ready, that person will know you're working toward a goal.

And finally, don't let a bad day get you down. Everybody has "down time" once in a while. Starting out in a career is always the hardest part. With patience and hard work, you should get where you want to be.

Many schools and communities offer theater groups for young people.

Josh Wheeler
444 Woodland Avenue
Springfield, Oregon 92345
(503) 555-8216

Objective   To obtain an entry-level position in theater production

Education   Denfeld High School, Springfield, Oregon, class of 1994

Experience   *Denfeld High School Theater*
             September 1992–June 1993, September 1993 to present
             Assisted backstage, building and painting sets. Also helped
             move scenery during productions.

             Highland Community Theater, Eugene, Oregon.
             Summer 1993
             Intern. Assisted stage manager with small tasks. Worked on
             scheduling: input schedules into computer, helped keep actors
             up-to-date on rehearsal schedules, ran errands.

             Other part-time jobs including mowing lawns, dog walking,
             and organizing neighborhood car washes.

Skills   Knowledge of computers.
             Ability to schedule and coordinate events.
             Experience in basic carpentry.

GLOSSARY

actor A person (man or woman) who portrays a character and gives it life. The character may be make-believe or based on a real person.

artistic director A person who determines what kinds of plays a theater company will present.

assistant casting director A person who assists the casting director.

assistant set designer A person who assists the set designer.

assistant stage manager A person who assists the stage manager.

backdrop A flat surface that is painted to represent the desired setting. Backdrops are usually made of canvas and wood.

blocking Determining the actors' basic movements in a play.

call To signal light, sound, and scenery changes during a theater performance. "Calling the show" is part of the stage manager's job.

callback A second or third audition. Callbacks narrow down the large number of actors who audition for one part.

casting director A person who helps cast the actors in a play.

choreograph To arrange or direct the movements and details of a staged fight scene, dance, etc.

choreographer A person who determines the movements and details of a dance.

cold reading An audition or part of an audition in which the actor is asked to read something he or she has never seen before.

costume designer A person who decides what the actors in a play will wear, and then designs those costumes.

director A person who is responsible for a production, including the actors and technical people. He or she is responsible for the interpretation of the script.

draper The person in the costume shop who makes the patterns from the costume designer's sketches.

fight director A person who coordinates the fight scenes in a play and teaches the movements to the actors.

fly system The system located above the stage (out of the audience's view) that lifts scenery clear of the stage.

footworks The foot movements of a fight scene or dance.

free-lance Type of work without long-term commitments to any one employer.

head shot An 8 inch × 10 inch black-and-white glossy photograph of an actor that is given to a casting director before or during an actor's audition.

lighting designer A person who designs the lights for a theater production.

load in To place the set on the stage where the play is to be performed.

onstage extra A person who appears on stage but has no lines.

picture boards Poster-size boards featuring pictures of various pieces of clothing. Some costume designers use picture boards to show the director what he or she is thinking of for the costumes.

playwright An author of a script.

producer A person who supervises or finances a theater production.

production meeting A meeting in which the people involved in a theater production discuss the technical aspects of the show.

prompt To assist an actor by saying the first few words of a line that he or she has forgotten.

property master A person who finds the props that will be used in a play and makes sure that those props are in the right place at the right time.

props Short for stage properties. The items you see on the set of a play.

regional theater A professional, nonprofit theater located away from a major theater center such as New York City.

rig To "fix" a costume so that it is easier to change into and out of.

run props To make sure that each prop is in the right place at the right time during a theater production.

scene shop A shop where scenery is built and painted.

scenic artist A person who works in a scene shop.

script The written text of a play, screenplay, radio or television broadcast.

seamstress/tailor A person who makes a living by sewing.

set carpenter A person who builds the set for a theater production.

set designer A person who designs the background for a theater production.

sides The parts of a script that contain a character's lines.

stage manager A person who coordinates the performance of a play from backstage. In professional theater, the responsibility of a production falls to the stage manager after opening night.

stock A collection of costumes, props, and other items in a regional theater.

stunt person A person who is trained to take the place of an actor in scenes that are dangerous, as in movies.

summer stock A theater that operates only during the summer. Some summer stock theaters are connected to universities, and some are professional.

technical rehearsals Rehearsals that are devoted to working out the technical aspects of a play.

touchstone piece A specific prop that represents the props as a whole.

understudy A person who is prepared to act another's part or take over another's duties.

wardrobe assistant A person who maintains the costumes for a theater production.

INDEX